Take the no-screen challenge

THE CALM WORKBOOK

A Kid's Activity Book for Relaxation and Mindfulness

Blow bubbles for moments of calm

Stretch and yawn to reset

Make a slime stress-reliever!

IMOGEN HARRISON

Foreword by Amanda Ashman-Wymbs,
BA (Hons) BACP accredited Counselor and Psychotherapist

Sky Pony Press
New York

T0020974

Copyright © 2022 by Summersdale Publishers Ltd.

First published as *The Calm Workbook* in the United Kingdom by Summersdale Publishers, an imprint of Octopus Publishing Book.

First Skyhorse edition, 2023.

All rights reserved. No part of this book may be reproduced in any manner without the express written consent of the publisher, except in the case of brief excerpts in critical reviews or articles. All inquiries should be addressed to Sky Pony Press, 307 West 36th Street, 11th Floor, New York, NY 10018.

Sky Pony Press books may be purchased in bulk at special discounts for sales promotion, corporate gifts, fund-raising, or educational purposes. Special editions can also be created to specifications. For details, contact the Special Sales Department, Sky Pony Press, 307 West 36th Street, 11th Floor, New York, NY 10018 or info@skyhorsepublishing.com.

Sky Pony® is a registered trademark of Skyhorse Publishing, Inc.®, a Delaware corporation.

Visit our website at www.skyponypress.com.

10 9 8 7 6 5 4 3 2 1

Manufactured in China, September 2022
This product conforms to CPSIA 2008

Library of Congress Cataloging-in-Publication Data is available on file.

Text by Poppy O'Neill
Interior and cover design by Summersdale Publishers Ltd.
US edition editor: Nicole Frail

Print ISBN: 978-1-5107-7321-9

Printed in China

This book belongs to...

_____

Contents

Foreword by Amanda Ashman-Wymbs, BA (Hons) BACP accredited Counselor and Psychotherapist ... 6

Welcome, parents and caregivers! ... 8

Hi there! ... 10

Let's talk ... 12

What it feels like to not feel calm ... 14

Fight, flee, or freeze? ... 16

Cool shades ... 18

Listen to your body ... 20

Name your feelings ... 22

Messy moments! ... 24

I FEEL COOL AS A CUCUMBER ... 28

Word soother ... 30

Dragon's breath ... 32

Positive self-talk ... 34

What are thoughts? ... 36

Think yourself calm ... 38

Shoo away the worry gremlins ... 40

Breathing shapes ... 42

I AM BRAVE ... 44

Bubble time ... 46

Go green ... 48

Mindful walking ... 50

Ground yourself ... 52

Have fun with fractals! ... 54

Mindful eating ... 56

Food rainbow ... 58

I AM HEALTHY AND STRONG! ... 60

Finding focus ... 62

Stretch to reset 64

Coping with change 66

Let it grow 68

Yawn! 70

Comfort zone 72

The Big Challenge Challenge!! 74

I FEEL CALM AND CONFIDENT 76

Make a box of calm 78

Keep on moving! 80

Soothing slime 82

Calming sparkle jar 84

Take a pencil for a walk 86

Just sing! 88

Power-down routine 90

The No-Screen Challenge 92

Time for a story 94

Make a reading den 96

Press the magic "pause" button 98

Super self-care ideas 100

I AM KIND 102

Cultivate kindness 104

Help others feel calm 106

Keep a gratitude journal 108

Spend time with a furry friend 110

Rain stick 112

Stay hydrated 114

I AM WORTHY OF GOOD THINGS 116

Five breaths to feeling calm 118

My calm tool kit 120

Conclusion 122

Final thoughts for parents and caregivers ... 124

FOREWORD

By Amanda Ashman-Wymbs,
BA (Hons) BACP accredited Counselor and Psychotherapist

Having worked with children therapeutically for a long time in schools and the private sector, and being a parent to two girls, it has become clear to me that helping children find their way back to a calm center within themselves is much-needed today. It can also have lasting value—way beyond childhood.

The Calm Workbook is a great resource for children, and it helps the caring adults around them support their journey from a state of anxiety and stress back to feeling calm again.

Written in simple language and packed with effective and fun activities, this workbook offers a friendly and holistic approach so a child can learn to understand and recognize what they may be experiencing internally, and why. There are also plenty of creative tips, techniques, and exercises to encourage calm and age-appropriate psychological techniques such as positive thinking, affirmations, and emotional literacy.

This book also demonstrates effective ways to improve mental and physical well-being and shows how to tune into and develop mindfulness by using breathwork, exploring our senses, and spending time in nature. These tools will support children in developing connections both inside and outside themselves.

I highly recommend this workbook for helping children feel calm and peaceful within.

Welcome,
parents and caregivers!

We all want our children to feel calm, happy, and composed, particularly when faced with a life of constant change and challenges, but the reality is that we all experience stress and worry from time to time—it's completely normal! When our children experience stress and worry, however, it can be difficult for them to understand and articulate it, which can in turn make it difficult to know how best to support them. Being able to calm oneself in any given situation is a valuable skill, and this book contains the tools for your child to learn how to self-soothe with trusted mindfulness and cognitive behavioral therapy techniques.

We'll look at how to help your child step out of their comfort zone with gentle step-by-step confidence-boosting challenges and positive self-talk, as well as learn some quick ways to calm themselves with fun, creative tasks. By the end of the book, your child will be able to create their very own calm tool kit that will set them up to be mentally strong and resilient for life.

You know your child best, and you may choose to work with them on the activities, but let them speak, and be careful not to influence their responses. The best way to support them is through active listening so that your child feels safe expressing themselves to you. Let them have their say and respond by using body language to show you are listening and understanding. When the moment's right, paraphrase what they have said, showing they have your full attention. You don't need to agree with your child—a lot of worries can seem irrational—but you can still affirm and empathize with them.

If your child would prefer not to write down or discuss specific thoughts, the same themes in the book can be explored through drawing and painting, role-playing games, building blocks, singing songs, dancing to music, or making mud pies—whatever captures your child's imagination. Research has found expressing difficult emotions through creative play is one of the most effective ways for children to process their feelings and improve their mental health.

Look out for the parent/caregiver and child icons, as these act as signals for more technical information about the relevance and usefulness of a specific activity.

HI THERE!

Welcome to your new calm and cool-as-a-cucumber activity book. This is the place where you will learn some amazing skills you can use for the rest of your life to help you manage difficult feelings and feel calmer, too, while having lots of fun along the way.

Being able to calm ourselves when faced with challenges or uncomfortable emotions is an important life skill. It gives us confidence to try new things and helps us feel happy, strong, and ready to take things on, knowing that we can soothe away our worries or negative thoughts.

Sometimes it can seem really hard to calm down. There are many reasons for this, and it's different for everyone.

**Here are some questions to ask yourself:
Do you often . . .**

- **get frustrated or upset when faced with a new situation or challenge?**

- **feel nervous when it's your turn to do something?**

- **find it hard to calm down when you're feeling big feelings?**

- **feel like everything is out of control?**

- **struggle to soothe your mind?**

If you're nodding your head while reading this list, then you've come to the right place. The good news is that there are lots of things you can do to help you feel calm, and this book is here to show you how—with the help of some fun challenges and activities, including making a rain stick and a sparkle jar, having fun with fractals, breathing exercises with shapes, and so much more.

By the end of the book, you will have your own personal calm tool kit—a list of things that work for you whenever you need a boost of courage or a reminder that you're unique and special.

Take your grown-up along for the ride, because there are special tips throughout for them to read with you if you'd like and activities that could be fun to do together!
Look for this icon for the special tips:

Let's start!

LET'S TALK

When we're not sure about something or feel nervous, worried, angry, or unhappy, talking to someone about it can really help us feel calm and in control again. On this page, draw your favorite people that you feel comfortable talking to.

If you don't feel confident about talking, you can always write a note.

Name: _____   Name: _____

Name: _____ **Name:** _____

What it feels like to not feel calm

In order to start feeling calm, we need to understand what's making us feel, uhm, not calm! The things that make us feel "not calm" are as unique to each of us as our fingerprints. Some of us have fears of certain objects or people or places, while others worry about the weather or the dark, and many of us worry about the same things, like taking a test, meeting new people, and being embarrassed in public. Or, maybe your reason for not feeling calm might be harder to pinpoint—it could just be a feeling in your tummy, and that's okay, too.

The important thing to remember in all of this is that it's normal to not feel calm sometimes, and there are some smart and fun ways to tame our worries and feel calm and in control again.

We all know what it feels like when we're not calm. It can be a range of physical sensations that look like this:

sad   dizzy   headache   hungry

hot

unable to concentrate   cold   tired

bad tempered

fast breathing   racing heart

butterflies in tummy   distracted

shivering

confused

sore tummy   stiff muscles

worried

Note: it's very rare to feel all these at once!

frustrated

14

Which ones do you feel when you're feeling worried, frightened, or angry—that is, not calm?

Draw them here and see if you can name your feelings.

15

Fight, flee, or freeze?

While we now know that not being calm doesn't feel very nice, these feelings can be useful since they keep us safe. The sudden panic that you feel is your body's alarm system. Humans have always had this, and in the past, having an inner alarm was very useful if you happened to come across a hungry bear or saber-toothed tiger while you were out minding your own business. These feelings produce a surge of adrenaline—a hormone that protects us from danger by making us feel strong and powerful and prepares your body to fight, flee, or freeze! Yes, we're still like our ancestors!

1 – FIGHT: a rush of energy in your body; the tensing muscles and rapid heart rate are designed to sharpen your senses to take on that saber-toothed tiger.

2 – FLIGHT: the same burst of energy prepares you to run away from the saber-toothed tiger and seek safety.

3 – FREEZE: this is the response when you have seen the saber-toothed tiger and you stay perfectly still in hopes that it hasn't spotted you.

Grrrr!

So which of these scenarios will make
you fight, flee, or freeze?

A shark takes a nibble on your surf board

_____

The hairdresser cuts too much off your fringe

_____

You've eaten a super-hot chili pepper

_____

It's time for show-and-tell and it's your turn

_____

Someone new comes over to say hello and asks
if they can play

_____

This book will help you regulate your alarm system with
some super-calm and super-cool skills!

COOL SHADES

You're going to need these
because you are a superstar!

Color in or decorate your favorites!

LISTEN TO YOUR BODY

You are unique and so are your needs. Sometimes you might want to be quiet and have time on your own, other times you might want to run around with your friends—it's okay to want different things at different times.

All humans need a healthy mix of the following things in their lives:

rest

exercise

time to concentrate

time to think

relaxation

play

connection with others

Always listen to your body and remember that you can ask for what you need, and what you need is allowed to change.

When you're feeling uncomfortable feelings,
ask yourself the following questions:

am I
thirsty?

am I
tired?

am I too
hot?

am I
hungry?

am I
lonely?

am I
too cold?

am I
confused?

am I
worried?

If any of these sound familiar to you, you know what to do! Reach
out to your grown-up and let them know how they can help.

NAME YOUR FEELINGS

Part of looking after yourself means being able to understand how you're feeling. This might sound silly, because it's usually obvious when you're happy or sad! But there are lots of other ways you can feel, too, and they're all different.

Naming your feelings is an important skill, because when you understand your emotions, it's much easier for you to find ways to feel better. For example, if you're confused, you could talk to your grown-up. If you're angry, you could try running or doing jumping jacks to help you calm down. If you're tired, you could take a nap or go to bed earlier.

Take a look at the feelings chart on the facing page and check beside the feeling or feelings you are experiencing right now.

	M	T	W	T	F	S	S
happy							
sad							
excited							
confused							
tired							
worried							
angry							
surprised							
calm							
disappointed							
nervous							
scared							
proud							
upset							
confident							
bored							

23

Messy moments!

We all have messy moments—when things go wrong or we make a mistake, or things simply don't work out the way we hoped they would. When we have messy moments, it can be tempting not to try those things ever again.

When stuff goes wrong, you need to remind yourself in big letters that:

Nobody is perfect!

and

You are great, just as you are!

And, in fact, messy moments can be very good for us because they help us remember:

- It's normal to make mistakes—everyone makes them, and I mean everyone!

- Getting a low mark in a test simply means that you need more practice.

- When you fix a problem, it shows that you can overcome a challenge, which will give you confidence to try even more difficult things!

- Even when things look bad, you can always find something good to be happy about.

- Trying things for the first time can be daunting, but every time you do something new, you grow as a person!

Keep these as reminders for when you have your next messy moment.

25

Help Messy Max find his way out of the Messy Maze

Word soother

Calming words can be soothing in times of need. Some people pick a special word to think or say out loud to help them feel calm. These words are called mantras. A mantra is a powerful word, phrase, or even a sound that can help you feel your best. When you repeat a mantra, either in your head or out loud, it can shape how you feel so you become confident in yourself and your abilities.

Think about some calming words you could use for a mantra and fill the clouds on this page with them. These calming words can help shape how you feel and behave.

I watch my worries float away

I feel calm

I am capable

I am loved

Relax

Dragon's breath

When we feel worried or uneasy, we tend to breathe more quickly and only take shallow breaths. This can make us feel worse inside because we're not inhaling enough oxygen to feel better. This is where your dragon can help you breathe more deeply and feel calm.

You will need

- A cardboard tube, or you can make a tube by rolling up a piece of card and fixing it securely.
- Red and yellow tissue paper, so your dragon can breathe fire!
- Scissors
- Sticky tape
- Glue and brush
- Torn pieces of paper from magazines or colored paper, to make your dragon's scaly body

1   Start by tearing up some colored paper or old magazines into roughly 1/2 inch squares, until you have a good handful of pieces.

2   Stand your tube on its end and dab glue on a small area and begin sticking the scales at an angle. Once you have covered the first small section, go on to the next, and keep going until your tube is covered.

32

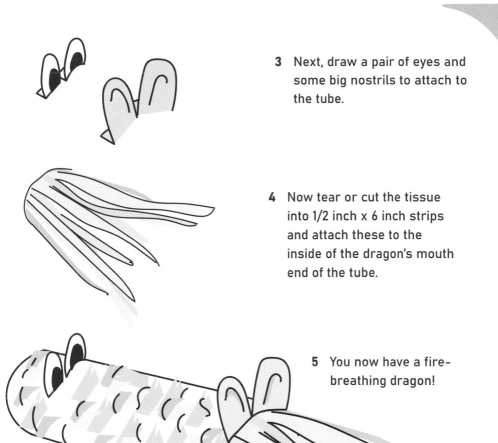

3 Next, draw a pair of eyes and some big nostrils to attach to the tube.

4 Now tear or cut the tissue into 1/2 inch x 6 inch strips and attach these to the inside of the dragon's mouth end of the tube.

5 You now have a fire-breathing dragon!

Breathe in deeply through your nose and blow out slowly through the tube so the flames dance out of the dragon's mouth. Try this a few times and see how much calmer you feel.

POSITIVE SELF-TALK

Positive self-talk is when we talk kindly to ourselves in a reassuring and helpful way. For example, imagine getting the results of a school test and discovering you didn't do as well as you'd hoped. It's easy to be hard on yourself, saying you should have done better. A more reassuring and kinder thing to say to yourself would be something like, "I tried my best and it's okay to make mistakes. I will keep trying and will do better next time."

Here is a list of positive affirmations that you might like to say to yourself.

I deserve happiness and kindness

I do my best

I am enough

I can do difficult things

I am strong

34

Take notice of the language of your thoughts and, next time you catch a negative one, try changing it to be positive. For instance:

Instead of:	Say this:
"This is too hard" or "I can't do this"	"This is hard, but I will try my best"
"I am helpless"	"I feel helpless, but I know that even small actions can make a difference"
"There is nothing I can do"	"I will do whatever I can do"

You could add some of your own, too!

What are thoughts?

That's a big question, isn't it? Is a thought a thing like a carrot or a mouse? Is it something you can smell, taste, see, hear, or feel? It's none of those things, because a thought is simply an idea that pops in your head, and ideas can't hurt you, can they?

We all have a zillion thoughts a day, some big and some small, some good and some bad. Often it's the bad ones that take up more space in our minds than the good ones, and these can be trouble, because they can make us worried or sad or any number of emotions.

When you have these troublesome feelings, you can disperse them by asking yourself two important questions:

1. How likely is it that this troubling thought will come true?

2. If it does come true, what can I do about it?

Write down your thoughts in the popcorn and then see if you can answer the two questions about each thought with your grown-up. It's likely that most of the time the thing you're most worried about will not happen, but if it does, you can handle it, and if you need extra support, your grown-up will be there for you.

37

THINK YOURSELF CALM

The brain is pretty powerful, and your thoughts are like a superpower! When dealing with difficult or uncomfortable thoughts, it can help to make a picture in your mind or "visualize" a place or situation that makes your brain feel calm, and this makes you relaxed, too. The reason visualization works is because your brain can interpret a happy thought as though it's real. Sounds amazing, doesn't it!

The key is to make the happy thought as real as possible in your mind. Here are some questions to help you visualize it:

How does it feel?

For example, is it a sunny place, so you can feel the warmth on your face? What does it feel like underfoot? Are there pebbles or grass or sand or water or a soft carpet?

How does it sound and what does it smell and taste like?

Are there food smells, like chocolate or fresh strawberries? Can you taste anything—a favorite food perhaps? Can you hear people talking or perhaps hear the wind in the trees or the waves lapping at the shore?

38

What can you see?

See if you can draw your happy place here.

Shoo away the worry gremlins

Worries can keep us awake at night or even make us feel on edge for a big part of our day. Sometimes when it's something in particular that's making us feel not right, it can be good to write those worries down, as it can make them seem less scary. If you work with your grown-up on this activity, they can help you work out which worries need the most attention, so that you can tackle them together one by one and find solutions for them.

Write your worries in the little worry gremlins' tummies.

If your worries are feeling too big to talk about right now, leave them for a bit and come back to them when you're feeling calm and strong.

41

BREATHING SHAPES

Paying attention to your breath while tracing a shape can help you slow your breath and calm yourself.

Try some of these breathing shapes and see which ones you like the best.

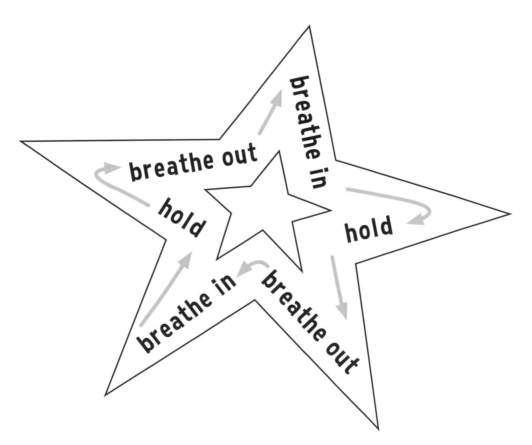

42

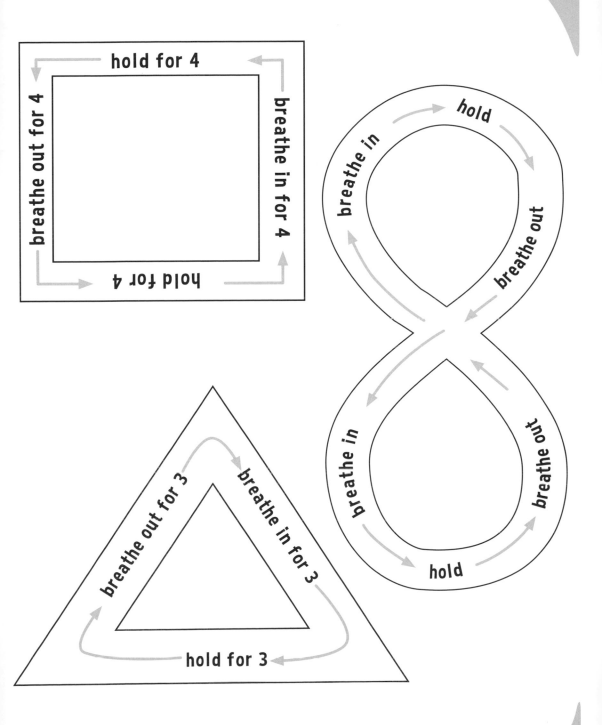

hold for 4

breathe out for 4

breathe in for 4

hold for 4

breathe in

hold

breathe out

breathe in

breathe out

hold

breathe out for 3

breathe in for 3

hold for 3

43

Bubble time

Uncomfortable feelings can sometimes feel a bit stuck, like hiccups, and are difficult to share because we might not have the words to explain them just yet. Blowing bubbles can help you to let go of these uncomfortable feelings and feel calm again.

Making bubbles is simple to do.

You will need

For the bubble wand:
- a piece of fuse wire or pipe cleaner

For the bubbles:
- A jelly jar
- Dish soap
- Glycerine*
- Water

*You can buy glycerine at supermarkets. If you don't have glycerine, you can use a few drops of vegetable oil or golden syrup instead.

1

Start by making a loop in the middle of your wire (or pipe cleaner) about the same size as the one pictured here.

2

Twist the two ends together to make the handle.

3

In your jelly jar, make a mixture that is 50 percent water and 50 percent dish soap and give it a stir. Then add a teaspoon of glycerine and mix this in. You can use your wand as the mixer!

4

You're now ready to blow bubbles and watch your troubles float away! Simply dip the loop of the wand into the mixture and blow your bubbles. Imagine these bubbles are your worries, lighter than air, as they float away on the breeze. Watch them pop and disappear.

GO GREEN

One of the best things you can do to make yourself feel great is simply go outside! Feel the sun on your cheeks—or maybe the rain—and listen to the wind in the trees. If you have a yard, take off your shoes and let the grass tickle your toes.

Whether you stay in your yard or go to a local park, field, or forest, going outside has been proven by scientists to make you feel better. It helps your mind and body relax and gives your mood a boost. See if your grown-up will join in and go barefoot, too!

There are so many things to do outside, it's impossible to count them all! You can sit still or run around—the choice is yours.

Here are just a few ideas to get you started:

Play catch

Gaze at the clouds

Watch for birds and wildlife

Smell the flowers

Design a natural obstacle course

Make a fairy garden

Have a water fight

Build a den

Make mud sculptures

Collect leaves,
flowers, or chestnuts

49

MINDFUL WALKING

You probably walk around every day without thinking about it, but did you know walking is actually a secret superpower that can help you feel calm?

When we feel anxious, we often feel as though we're trapped in our own head. Mindful walking is a simple way to feel better because it makes you focus on the present moment while your body is moving—and this gets rid of the trapped feeling.

To try mindful walking, find a quiet spot. It could be in your living room or in the garden. If you like, take off your shoes and socks so you're standing barefoot (make sure there are no sharp objects to step on before you start). Take a few deep breaths and tune into your toes and what you can feel. Is it soft carpet? Cool tiles? Fluffy grass? Next, take a slow step forward. Feel your leg as it moves, and notice all the muscles working hard to lift your foot. Then, slowly place your foot down in front of you. Keep walking back and forth, thinking about your body as it moves.

What sensations did you notice? Draw or write them on the clouds on the next page.

By noticing what your body is feeling,
and paying attention to the movement
of your arms and legs, you are focusing
on the present moment.

GROUND YOURSELF

If you're feeling anxious, there is a simple activity you can try called grounding. Grounding is a way of making a special connection between you and something natural, and it helps you find a feeling of calm.

There are different ways to ground yourself.
Here are some ideas:

My favorite spot
Pick somewhere outdoors that you love and that you can get to easily. It could be in your yard, somewhere at school, or in a local park. Once you have chosen your spot, sit there as often as you can and notice the things around you. Can you see signs of the seasons changing? Is there any wildlife? It won't take long before you know this spot really well, and it will be your own special place to visit whenever you need some quiet time. (If your special place is in the park, you will need to ask your grown-up to take you.)

Hug a tree

Try giving a tree a big hug! Rest your face on the trunk and feel the texture of the bark. Close your eyes and imagine the roots reaching down into the earth and the branches high in the sky. Maybe you're lucky enough to have a tree in your yard that you can hug every day. If not, perhaps you will pass one on the way to school, or you can find a favorite tree in your local park.

Go barefoot

Walking with no shoes and socks on is a great way to feel connected with nature. As long as the ground is safe and there's nothing sharp, you can walk on any surface you like, whether it's grass, brick, sand, or mud. The bottoms of your feet are very sensitive, so they can feel all the different textures of the ground as you go. You could walk barefoot with your grown-up and talk about the things you're feeling.

Have fun with fractals!

Science has shown that studying the patterns in nature has such a calming effect on the brain that it can reduce stress levels by up to 60 percent.

Have you ever looked closely at the furry body of a honeybee or the delicate patterns on a butterfly's wing, or even the map-like intricate beauty of a leaf skeleton? Focusing on the fascinating details of the natural world is not only fun but calming, too!

Try some of these ideas:

Find some long grasses and braid them.

Look for the weirdest and most wonderful mushrooms and fungi and take pictures so you can sketch them in detail when you get home.

See how many different colors and shades of fallen leaves you can find and arrange them into a rainbow or make a collage of a woodland animal with them.

Take some paper and wax crayons
into the woods or your yard and make
bark rubbings on the paper.

Admire a caterpillar under a magnifying glass.

Watch ants as they go about their
business. Where do they go?

What other ideas can you come up with to study the tiny
and beautiful patterns in nature? Add your ideas here.

Mindful eating

Eating is another thing you probably do without really thinking about it. But when you slow down and pay attention to what your senses are telling you, you will notice so much more.

This is called mindful eating. Try it next time you have a meal. When your food is in front of you, tune into everything your senses are experiencing. What does your food look like? What does it smell like? When you take a bite, close your eyes to help you notice small details. How would you describe the taste? What does it feel like? You could try this with your grown-up and talk about what you noticed.

No two foods taste the same. Isn't that amazing? Everything you eat will have a unique flavor, smell, and texture. Some foods even have sounds. Think of the crunch of toast or the snap of a carrot stick. Use this page to draw the things you've eaten mindfully and write down one detail about each one.

Food rainbow

What are your favorite foods? Do you wish you could eat them every day, for every meal? Your body needs lots of different foods to grow strong and healthy, so having your favorites three times a day would make you feel tired and possibly make you ill!

To feel your best and be your strongest, you need a whole rainbow of foods. Can you draw different foods for each of the colors of the rainbow?

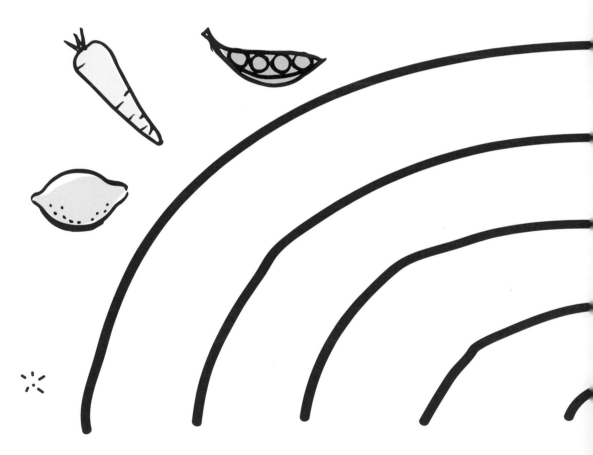

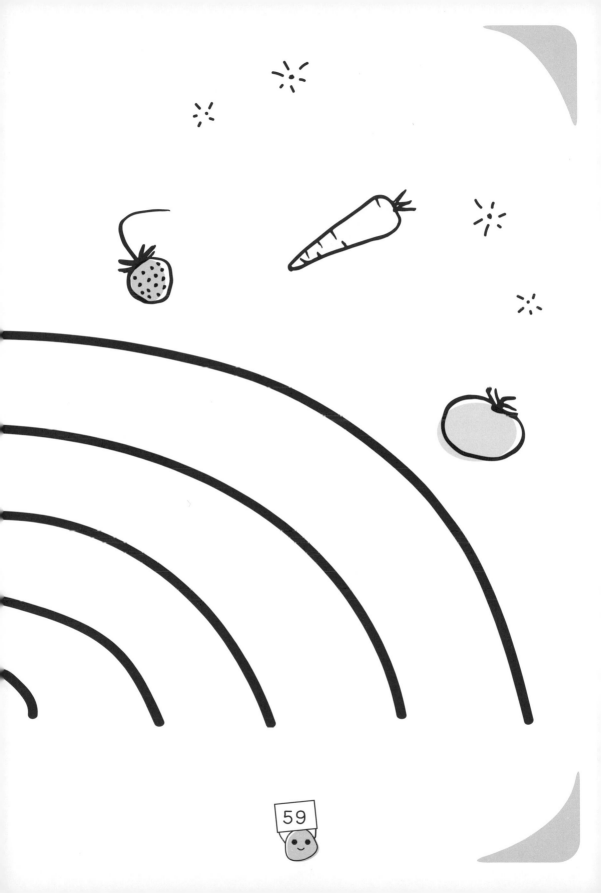

59

Finding focus

You are more than worry or anger or frustration—you are more than any of the moods that you experience. Even with worry, you can be brave, and even when you're angry or upset, there is always something good to smile about.

What are the things that make you the strong, brave, and kind person you are? Here's a fun quiz to find out what makes you uniquely you!

What makes you a good friend?
Circle the words that best describe you.

loyal   caring   good listener

friendly   funny

good joke teller

kind   smart

What are your favorite hobbies . . .

. . . with a ball?

_____

. . . with art supplies?

_____

. . . with your friends?

_____

Name three surprising skills you have.

1. _____
2. _____
3. _____

I make the best salad wraps. Yum yum!

What's the kindest thing you could say to yourself?

I'm great because . . .

_____

What are the challenges that you have overcome and thought WOW?

1. _____
2. _____
3. _____
4. _____
5. _____

What's your biggest achievement from the past 12 months?

_____

STRETCH TO RESET

If you're feeling uneasy, try having a stretch. When you stretch, it sends a signal to your heart to pump blood to your muscles, which makes them feel good. Stretching can also make your body release hormones called endorphins, which make you feel happy.

Try these simple stretches, and enjoy the feeling of being a tree, a butterfly, and a fish.

Tree

Lift your arms up over your head and reach toward the sky. Try to touch the clouds! Then, gently lean to one side, like a tree bending in the wind. You will feel a stretch all down one side of your body. Hold your position for a few seconds, then lean to the other side. Hold again for a few seconds and then relax.

Butterfly

First, sit comfortably on the ground. Then put the soles of your feet together and hold onto your ankles. Each leg is now like a butterfly's wing! You should feel a stretch down the top of your legs. If you want to, gently lean forward to stretch your back, as well. Hold your position for a few seconds and then relax.

Fish

Find a comfortable place to sit with your legs out in front of you. Keep your back as straight as you can, and let your shoulders relax. Then, reach toward your toes so that you're folded forward. You should feel a stretch down the backs of your legs. Hold your position for a few seconds and then relax.

Remember: it doesn't matter if you can only bend a little way—you will still feel great afterwards!

A stretch should always feel comfortable, so listen to your body. If anything hurts, stop and tell your grown-up.

Coping with change

Change can make us feel uneasy and worried, but there are things you can do to feel calm when it happens. Change is part of life—you could be going to a new school, moving to a new house, or welcoming a new family member, for example. Having some mindful techniques for these times will help you feel calm. Try these quick calmers with your grown-up and see how they make you feel.

FOUR SENSES

This is as simple as it sounds. The idea is to sit quietly and notice four things around you.

Sit with your grown-up on a comfy sofa or rug.

Each person takes turns telling the other person something that they can:

See   **Hear**   **Smell**   **Touch**

THE LISTENING GAME

We have all played the quiet game before—where you try to be silent for as long as you can. This is slightly different, as you need to concentrate on what you can "hear" as well as being silent and still. Play it with your grown-up at home.
They can set a timer for 1 minute.

While you're being silent for 1 minute, see how many different noises you can hear—even really quiet ones like the creak of a floorboard in another room or a bird on a branch outside the window.

When your grown-up tells you the minute is up, see how many things you can recall that you heard and recount them. To make it even more fun, you could both play and write your findings down on a piece of paper once the time is up and see who has heard the most individual noises.

These exercises are a great way for you and your grown-up to connect in a different way and will help you build tools to center yourself and feel calm.

LET IT GROW

Have you ever watched something grow from a tiny seed into a plant? Growing a plant is a very calming project. Plants take their time to grow, and there's nothing you can do to rush them. This means that when you garden, you have to be calm, patient, and slow, just like the plant.

There are lots more wonderful feelings to be gained from growing a plant. You can engage all your senses: see the rich colors of leaves, feel cool earth on your fingers, smell the beautiful fragrance of a flower, listen to the trickle of the water in the watering can, and, if you choose an edible plant, perhaps you will even taste the things that you grow. It's also exciting to see a plant growing because, every time you see it, you can be proud of what you've achieved!

Ask your grown-up to help you prepare a small patch of your garden or set up some pots indoors. Here are some plants that are great fun to grow:

Strawberries

Sweet peas

Lettuce

Peas

Flowers

Plant a seed or seedling and use the page below to draw
your plant week by week. How much has it grown?
Does it have new leaves?

Week 1	Week 2	Week 3	Week 4
Week 1	Week 2	Week 3	Week 4
Week 1	Week 2	Week 3	Week 4
Week 1	Week 2	Week 3	Week 4
Week 1	Week 2	Week 3	Week 4

Yawn!

When you're stressed, your muscles tend to tense up, which can make you feel even more yucky and not want to do anything. Here's a quick and effective way to reset and feel better, and all you have to do is yawn!

Several times a day, spend a few minutes stretching out any physical tension to ease both your body and mind with a yawn!

blink a few times

stretch those arms

yawn!

wiggle your fingers

stretch your neck like a tortoise

shake a leg

Hug!

Simple but immediately effective, a hug will lower blood pressure, boost your immune system, and leave you feeling happier.

Physical contact is scientifically proven to lower blood pressure and boost levels of oxytocin (the "love hormone") in the body. A quick hug from a loved one or friend could be a great calming influence.

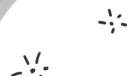

Comfort zone

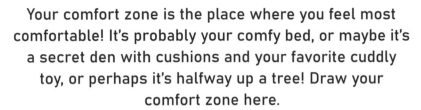

Your comfort zone is the place where you feel most comfortable! It's probably your comfy bed, or maybe it's a secret den with cushions and your favorite cuddly toy, or perhaps it's halfway up a tree! Draw your comfort zone here.

A comfort zone also includes the things that you enjoy doing because you know you're good at them. Draw or write down the things that you're good at and you like doing. It can be anything: riding a bike, drawing beetles, peeling apples, taking photos, algebra!

Growing your comfort zone and trying things that you aren't currently comfortable doing or are new to you can be hard and worrying and make you feel all the feelings you have when you're not calm.

But the best thing about growing your comfort zone is that you will have more and more things in it that you can do and feel comfortable with. These could be things like picking up a pet to bigger things like talking to your class about your favorite pet!

When faced with a new thing, it's best to break it down into manageable stages. Here's an example:

Picking up a pet

Step 1: say hello to the pet from a distance

Step 2: offer it a treat to nibble off your hand or take from your fingers

Step 3: give it a gentle stroke (not if it's a fish!)

Step 4: sit beside someone who is holding the pet

Step 5: ask the person with the pet to place it in your lap

THE BIG CHALLENGE CHALLENGE!!

Now it's your turn to break down something big in your head into manageable steps so you can blast out of your comfort zone in your very own rocket!

1

2

3

75

Make a box of calm

When we need help relaxing and feeling calm, certain things can help us. These will be different for everyone; they might include pictures, a squeezy toy, a piece of soft fabric, a lucky stone, a favorite quote, a journal for writing down thoughts . . . whatever works for you. Why not decorate a shoebox and keep the objects that help you feel relaxed and confident in there? That way, they're all in one place whenever you need them.

What kind of things would go in your calm box? Write a list before you start gathering objects to go in there.

KEEP ON MOVING!

Physical exercise raises the heart rate and burns away excess adrenaline, the fizzy feeling in your tummy. It also prompts your brain to release endorphins, which make you feel happy. Physical exercise doesn't just keep you physically fit and healthy, but also keeps your mind healthy, too. What this means is that by playing sports every day, you are less likely to struggle with uncomfortable feelings like worry or fear. Here are some exercises to try out. See which ones you like best.

SKIPPING CYCLING WALKING skateboarding JUMPING DANCING games ball RUNNING yoga SWIMMING

80

What other things do you like to do to get your body moving? Write them here.

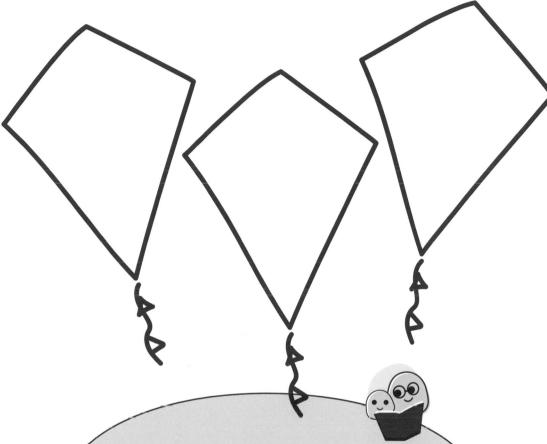

Any physical exercise that raises your heart rate is good for your health and helps you feel calmer. This is because exercise burns away excess adrenaline in your body, making it less likely that you will experience those uncomfortable feelings when faced with a new or challenging situation.

Soothing slime

Did you know you can take your mind off your worries with squishy, stretchy, squeezy slime? Here is an easy recipe for fluffy slime. Ask your grown-up to help you find the ingredients and have fun making it together.

You will need

- 5 ounces liquid glue
- $3/4$ teaspoon baking soda
- 5 tablespoons shaving cream
- Gel food coloring
- 1 teaspoon contact lens cleaning solution

1. Add the glue and baking soda into a bowl and mix well.

2. Then add the shaving cream and mix it in. (You can add more if you want extra-fluffy slime!)

3. Add a drop of food coloring and stir until combined.

4. Add the contact lens solution and mix. Keep going until the slime starts to come away from the bowl. Then knead it until it becomes smoother. It will be very sticky at first.

5. Your slime is ready to enjoy! When you've finished playing, store it in an airtight container.

6. You can add extra things to your slime, too! How about adding beads or foam balls to give it a cool crunchy texture, or some glitter to make it sparkle?

CALMING
SPARKLE JAR

Who doesn't love glitter?! A sparkle jar is like a snow globe but with glitter inside it. It can help you feel calm instantly. Simply give it a shake and place it on a surface. Then take a moment to watch the glitter sparkle and gently fall and settle to the bottom of the jar. As the glitter settles, you will feel calmer again. Here's how to make one:

1. **Find a glass jar with a screw-top lid. Give it a clean in warm water.**

2. **Decorate the jar on the outside with tissue paper or glass paint, if you have it, and leave to dry.**

3. **Once dry, fill the jar with water, then add 2 teaspoons of eco-friendly glitter in any color you like.**

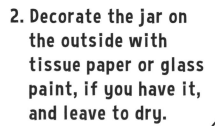

4. Glue around the inner rim of the lid and screw it on top of the jar. Allow it to dry.

5. Your glitter jar is ready to use. Give it a shake and watch the glitter float and fall.

Keep your glitter jar in a safe place so you can use it whenever you are feeling worried or upset. Imagine all the specks of glitter are your individual thoughts whizzing around your brain, so that when they settle to the bottom of the jar, you feel more settled, too.

TAKE A PENCIL
FOR A WALK

When you allow your mind to wander, it can help you reset and feel calm again. Take a pencil for a walk on this page. What do you notice? How many squirrels can you find? And how many different kinds of flowers are there? Where's the best picnic spot?!

87

Just sing!

Singing makes us happy: not only are there the physical benefits of deeper breaths, which boost our oxygen intake, but there's the release of those endorphins again. When you're concentrating on making music, your mind is distracted from your worries. You could have a sing-along playlist for the car or learn some campfire songs along with the actions.

What's on your sing-along playlist?

89

Power-down routine

Sleep is an amazing thing. While you're asleep, your body is busy growing and healing, and your brain is organizing your memories and processing information, as well as re-energizing for the next day. Getting enough sleep means that you can concentrate better, you have more energy, and you're more likely to feel calm and happy.

To get a good night's sleep, it often helps to do a few calming things before bedtime. There are lots of ideas below that you could try. Have a look at these and ask your grown-up to help you choose a few:

Have a hot drink

Take a bath

Read a book

Write in a journal

Quiet breathing

Relaxing stretches

Write down the things you've tried here, and have fun experimenting! When you find things you like, you can create a calming bedtime routine to do every night.

THE NO-SCREEN CHALLENGE

Do you watch a lot of TV? Or do you spend time looking at a screen? Although it's fun to watch programs and play games sometimes, spending lots of time looking at a screen can leave you feeling tired and overwhelmed. You might find that your muscles get sore when you've been sitting in one position for too long, as well.

Try the No-Screen Challenge for a week and see how you feel afterward. If you usually watch TV when you get home from school, do something else instead. Why not try one of the activities from this book, like making slime or planting a seed? If you like to play video games after dinner, choose a different activity instead to help you wind down before bed. You could listen to music, read a book, or have a bubble bath. By the end of the week, you might notice that you feel calmer and happier.

Write down how you feel after every day doing the No-Screen Challenge:

Monday:	
Tuesday:	
Wednesday:	
Thursday:	
Friday:	
Saturday:	
Sunday:	

Did you know?

The bright lights from screens make it more difficult to get to sleep as the "blue light" tricks the brain into thinking it's daytime. If you're struggling to get to sleep, try turning off screens at least an hour before bedtime.

Time for a story

Reading is very good for you as well as being great fun and sparking your imagination. Scientists have found that children who read stories are generally happier, as it exercises the mind in the same way as positive thinking. It also makes us calm by reducing stress levels. What are your favorite stories? Write them here in the pages of this open book.

Color in and cut out this Do Not Disturb sign.
Then tape it to the outside of your reading den
(turn the page to see how to make a den)!

DO NOT DiSTURB

I'm reading

96

Make a reading den

The best place to read is in your own secret reading den. It's quick and easy to make, and it will allow you to escape into your story without interruptions.

You will need

- A bed sheet
- Cushions
- Rugs
- Lots of imagination and possibly a few thumbtacks and clothes pins!

Find your cozy spot—it could be a window area, or a corner of your bedroom, or maybe the sofa. Find as many cushions as you can and maybe a chair or two to make a frame for your den so you can place your sheet over the top. Ask a grown-up to help with any heavy lifting!

Decorate the inside of your den with comfy cushions, a pile of your favorite books, and a toy. Use a flashlight or lantern if you need more light for reading.

PRESS THE MAGIC "PAUSE" BUTTON

Your body is very clever, and it can do lots of things at the same time—you can be walking, breathing, looking, feeling, hearing, and thinking all at once! But having so much going on in your body can sometimes feel overwhelming, especially when you're anxious. When you feel like this, try pressing the magic "pause" button.

All you need to do to press the magic "pause" button is find somewhere quiet and comfortable to sit. Ask your grown-up to give you a 2-minute timer. Then close your eyes and imagine that you're pressing a button in front of you. When you press it, let your body relax and allow whatever is on your mind to drift away. Feel your arms and legs go heavy. Listen to yourself breathing in and out. When your 2 minutes are up, open your eyes, stretch your arms and legs, and you should be feeling calmer and happier.

Write down some quiet places where you can go to press your magic "pause" button, or draw your dream quiet place.

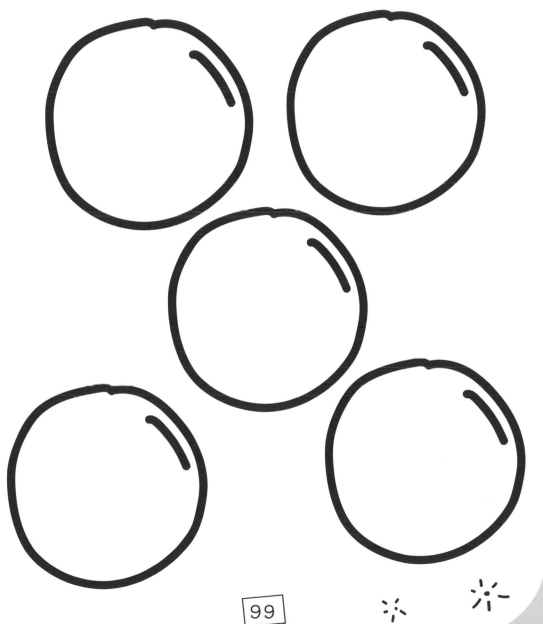

99

Super self-care ideas

You might have heard people talking about self-care, but what is it? Self-care is anything you do that helps keep you feeling happy, calm, and healthy. Taking a break when you feel overwhelmed is one way to look after yourself. Making time to do your favorite thing— whether that's running, dancing, singing, or reading—is self-care, as well, because when you do the things you love, it makes you happy.

If you're feeling anxious or worried, here are some simple self-care ideas to try:

Read a book

Do some coloring

Have a mini dance party

Try some gentle breathing exercises

Say some positive affirmations

Spend some time outdoors

Drink some water

Have a nap

Write down your favorite self-care ideas here:

Cultivate kindness

Kindness is about giving your time and care freely. It can be done in small ways, such as helping someone when they drop something or offering words of encouragement or just listening to someone who might need to talk about something that's important to them.

If we spread kindness into the world, it spreads happiness to those around us. Being kind to others can help us take our minds off our own troubles and gives a feeling of togetherness and support.

If you're kind to others, you'll find it easier to treat yourself kindly, which is very important in order to feel calm and happy within ourselves.

What kind things could you do today? Here are some ideas:

Smile more – Smiling is contagious and gives everyone around you an instant happiness boost.

Wishing others well – Send kind thoughts by speaking them out loud as affirmations.

Give a compliment a day – It could be to a friend, a family member or even a teacher. You'll make their day.

Put yourself in someone else's shoes – This means thinking about what it must be like to be feeling the way someone else is feeling.

104

Perform acts of kindness –
This could be anything that
would make another person feel
cared for: picking up litter in
a neighbor's yard, tidying your
room, writing a shopping list,
picking flowers to
give to someone who
might need
cheering up . . .

Think about some kind
things that you could do
for the people you know
and write them down here.

HELP OTHERS FEEL CALM

Sometimes when people aren't feeling calm and strong, they can show all sorts of emotions. Here are just a few:

Loud   **Angry**   **Quiet**

Frustrated   **Upset**   **Worried**

How many of these feelings do you recognize when you're not feeling calm? Can you think of any more? Write them here.

So what can we do to help others when they're not feeling calm?

Listen to their worries.

Look at them to see how they're feeling and show that you're listening.

Ask them if they're okay and if you can help.

Try one of the mindfulness exercises in this book together.

Show understanding.

Learning to understand how others are feeling and offering support is a great way to grow emotional intelligence. Practice role-playing a situation with your grown-up where one of you is feeling worried or frustrated and the other must try the prompts above to help them.

Keep a gratitude journal

Seeking out the good things in your life and writing them down in a daily journal is a great habit to get into, as it serves as a reminder that life is wonderful and exciting and no two days are the same! What sorts of things come to mind when you think about what makes you grateful to be you? It could be time you spend with a friend or your family, or something you are proud of. There is no rule as to how big or small these things that make you feel good should be.

Fill in the gratitude diary pages here. Start by adding the date to each entry so you can look back on each day and be reminded of the things you're thankful for. Make this part of your bedtime routine so you can reflect on the good experiences you've had during the day.

Journaling is a wonderful habit, as you gain wisdom from reflecting on your everyday experiences as well as a happy and calm feeling when you're reminded of all the good things in your life. People who focus on the good things tend to achieve more and feel much less stressed. Many studies have shown the positive effects of this, but one in particular shows that practicing gratitude causes changes in the brain that allow us to perform better when faced with new challenges.*

* Source: McCraty and Childre, "The Grateful Heart: The Psychophysiology of Appreciation" (2004)

Date	I am grateful for...

SPEND TIME WITH A FURRY FRIEND

Spending time with a pet is great fun—for you and the pet! Whether you have a guinea pig, a rabbit, a cat, or a dog, or maybe something more unusual, like a snake or gecko, petting an animal can make you feel happy and calm. This is because when you have the responsibility of looking after another living thing and its well-being and happiness, you feel their happiness, too. Knowing you have the skills to keep another living thing safe and well is a wonderful confidence booster! In addition, cuddling a pet helps you feel comforted, and pets can be very good listeners!

If you don't have a pet of your own, though, you can always spend time with other people's pets (with the owner's permission, of course) or perhaps your school has a pet you can help care for.

What would be your perfect pet? Answer these questions to find out and then draw it on the facing page.

What do they eat?

What sort of noise do they make?

Do they need to go for a walks?

Do they have fur, feathers, or fins?

Can they fit in your pocket?

What will you name them?

Are they cuddly?

Are they bigger than you?

What color are they?

110

Having a pet has been proven
to have many benefits to a young
person's self-esteem and self-confidence.
This is due to the interaction and
reciprocal nature of having an emotional
connection with an animal and being
part of its everyday care, well-being,
and development.

RAIN STICK

The sound of rain is very soothing to many, especially when you're watching it from a cozy spot indoors. You can make your own rain sounds with a rain stick for instant calm whenever you need it. Here's how to make one. This is an activity to do with your grown-up.

You will need

- A long cardboard tube (a poster tube works well)
- Hammer and panel pins or nails
- 1 pound dried beans, lentils or pasta
- Pieces of card or lids to cover the ends
- Colored paper for decoration
- Glue
- Scissors

1. Use the hammer to tap the pins into the cardboard tube at random intervals; these will slow the flow of the beans, making the rain sound!

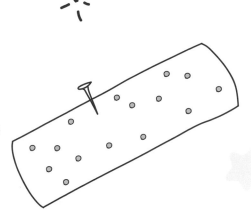

2. When you have finished, it should look something like this when you look down the tube. The more pins or nails you add, the longer your rainstorm will last!

3. Close up one end of the rain stick securely with either a lid or some card and tape.

4. Next, fill the container with your dried beans. You'll get your first rainstorm sounds by doing this!

5. Close the second end securely with a lid or card.

6. Decorate the outside of the rain stick with colored paper and whatever crafty bits you have lying around. Now tilt it and listen to the rain—while you stay warm and dry!

Stay hydrated

We all need water to survive, and not only that, being well hydrated will improve your mood and helps you stay focused and calm. Children ages 8 to 12 should be drinking around 8 cups of water a day. This can seem quite a lot, but there are some things you can do to make sure you stay hydrated throughout the day. The key is to drink before you're thirsty.

Drinking water on its own can be a bit boring, so why not add a fun twist to your drink with these ideas:

- Add a slice of lemon or orange, or a strawberry.

- Place chopped-up mint leaves, edible flowers, or soft fruits into ice cube trays, fill with water, and freeze. These can be added to your drink for extra flavor and interest—it's like a party in your drink!

- Eat vegetables high in water content for a juicy snack, such as cucumbers and celery sticks.

- Make your water bottle into a masterpiece by customizing it with stickers.

Don't forget to drink more when you're doing sports and exercise, and on hot days!

Color in the bottles for each day to show that you are staying fully hydrated!

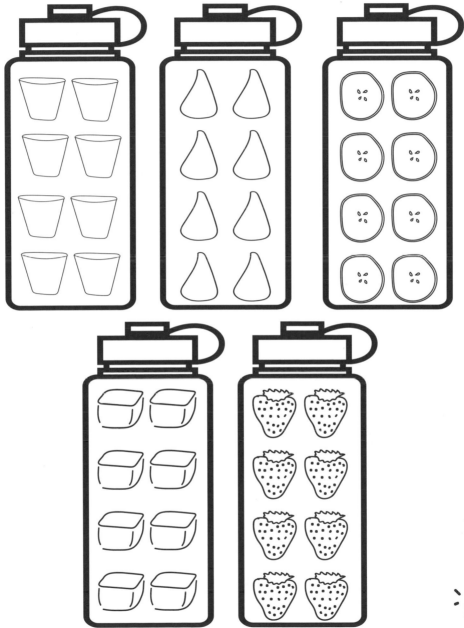

Five breaths to feeling calm

Mindful breathing is one of the simplest ways to help you feel calm and relaxed. It also helps you focus on the present moment rather than worrying about something in the future.

1. **Stand still with your feet slightly apart. Look down at your tummy and place your hand on it.**

2. Now breathe in and watch and feel your tummy inflate like a balloon.

3. Hold your breath to a count of three (if you can!).

4. Exhale slowly and feel your tummy shrink.

5. Repeat the process for four more breaths and see if you can make your tummy balloon a little bigger each time.

There are many ways to make mindful breathing simple and fun. Just experiment until you find your favorite.

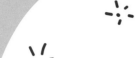

My calm toolkit

Here's your personal toolkit that you can use whenever you want to calm yourself.

Circle the activities below that work best for you, then make up your unique toolkit on the facing page.

When I need to feel calm, I can:

Breathe

Pause

Talk to my grown-up

Get moving

Write down my worries

Keep a gratitude journal

Hydrate

Be kind to myself

Yawn

Try visualization

Be kind to others

Use my rain stick or my glitter jar

Conclusion

Hopefully the skills you've learned in this book should go a long way to helping you feel calmer so you can cope better in times of difficulty. Knowing that you can calm yourself when you're worried, or being able to take on challenges by making small, manageable steps to reach your goal, or simply yawning to reset are skills that will be useful for your whole life.

Don't forget: the more you practise these skills, the calmer you'll be! You are cool and confident— give yourself a cheer!

Color in then cut out and keep these medals as a reminder of how great you are!

I AM BRAVE

I AM STRONG

I AM UNIQUE

I AM CALM

I AM KIND

Final thoughts for parents and caregivers

I hope the activities in this book have been fun and inspiring, and your child can use their newfound skills to self-soothe. There is no one-size-fits-all solution to regulating moods, because every human mind is different.

Here are some final thoughts to consider:

Keep talking to your child and talk through their feelings, both good and bad. This way, they'll find it easier to deal with normal levels of low mood or difficult experiences when they arise and will know how to recognize and ask for help if they feel overwhelmed.

If you feel that your child's low mood is having a negative effect on their daily life, it could be a good time to seek support outside the family. Start by talking to your child's school teacher or doctor. They'll be able to advise the next steps. Alternatively, you could go directly to a therapist to discuss your concerns. Involve your child in decision-making, listen to any concerns they have, validate, and reassure them. Treat it just as you would if you were seeking advice for a physical health symptom. Remember: seeking support is a sign of strength and love, and you should never feel guilt or shame for doing so.

When your child is struggling with their feelings, it can take a lot out of you. Make sure you have plenty of support, too. It can be hard to ask for help initially, but just know that those who care about you will want to help and be there for you.

Keep going! You're doing great!

Other Titles in the Big Feelings, Little Workbooks series...

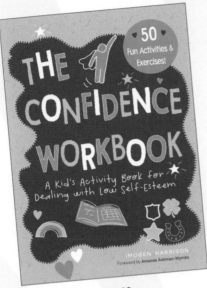

$16.99
Paperback
ISBN: 978-1-5107-7274-8

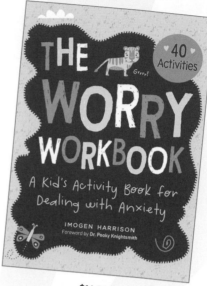

$16.99
Paperback
ISBN: 978-1-5107-6407-1

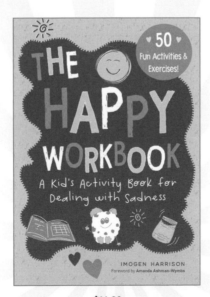

$16.99
Paperback
ISBN: 978-1-5107-7061-4

Look for these other helpful titles from Sky Pony Press!

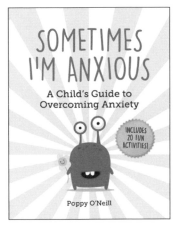

SOMETIMES I'M ANXIOUS

A Child's Guide to Overcoming Anxiety

INCLUDES 20 FUN ACTIVITIES!

Poppy O'Neill

Paperback
ISBN: 978-1-5107-4748-7

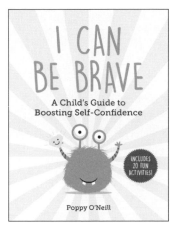

I CAN BE BRAVE

A Child's Guide to Boosting Self-Confidence

INCLUDES 20 FUN ACTIVITIES!

Poppy O'Neill

Paperback
ISBN: 978-1-5107-6408-8

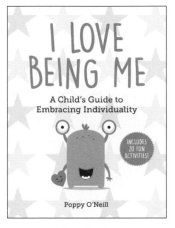

I LOVE BEING ME

A Child's Guide to Embracing Individuality

INCLUDES 20 FUN ACTIVITIES!

Poppy O'Neill

Paperback
ISBN: 978-1-5107-6409-5

BELIEVING IN ME

A Child's Guide to Self-Confidence and Self-Esteem

INCLUDES 30 FUN ACTIVITIES!

Poppy O'Neill

Paperback
ISBN: 978-1-5107-4747-0

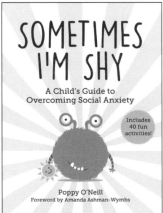

SOMETIMES I'M SHY

A Child's Guide to Overcoming Social Anxiety

Includes 40 fun activities!

Poppy O'Neill
Foreword by Amanda Ashman-Wymbs

Paperback
ISBN: 978-1-5107-7062-1

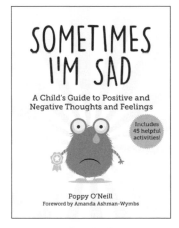

SOMETIMES I'M SAD

A Child's Guide to Positive and Negative Thoughts and Feelings

Includes 45 helpful activities!

Poppy O'Neill
Foreword by Amanda Ashman-Wymbs

Paperback
ISBN: 978-1-5107-7273-1

Image credits:

Cover, p.3 and throughout – fun icons © Wanchana365/Shutterstock.com; p.4 and throughout – firework © Lightkite/Shutterstock.com; p.10 and throughout – smiley faces © Cube29/Shutterstock.com; pp.12–13 – picture frames © Maaike Boot/Shutterstock.com; pp.14–15, 21, 40-41 © Daniela Barreto/Shutterstock.com; pp.16–17 – tiger © Solmariart/Shuttterstock.com; prehistoric people © notkoo/Shutterstock.com; pp.18–19 – glasses © By Anastacia - azzzya/Shutterstock.com; p.24 – splats © Alexey Pushkin/Shutterstock.com; pp.36–37, 44 © lineartespilot/Shutterstock.com; pp.48–49 © Kamieshkova/Shutterstock.com; pp.52–53 © Retany/Shutterstock.com; pp. 54–55 leaves © mirro/Shutterstock.com; ants © stockvit/Shutterstock.com; snail © Seja aka Lita/Shutterstock.com; p.57 © Aleksandrs Bondars/Shutterstock.com; pp.58–59 – fruit and veg © zabavina/Shutterstock.com; pp.60–61 © Elena Pimukova/Shutterstock.com; p.63 – medal © Goshantosa/Shutterstock.com; pp.64–65 © redchocolate/Shutterstock.com; p.70 – yawn © victor brave/Shutterstock.com; p.71 – hug © Lemonade Serenade/Shutterstock.com; p.73 © V_ctoria/Shutterstock.com; pp.74–75 © Art Alex/Shutterstock.com; p.76 – hot-air balloon, rainbow and bird © nataka/Shutterstock.com; p.82 © dbavan/Shutterstock.com; p.83 © ElenaProf/Shutterstock.com; pp.86–87 © isabirova/Shutterstock.com; pp.88–89 © Vectorry_music notes/Shutterstock.com; p.91 © Croisy/Shutterstock.com; p.94 © Airin.dizain; p. 115 – bottle © Sonia/Shutterstock.com; pp.116–117 © BNP Design Studio-outline/Shutterstock.com; p.121 © AVICON/Shutterstock.com; p.123 © Goshantosa/Shutterstock.com; all other images by Julie Goldsmith